to Lyndell Leatherman

Prelude on Come Share the Lord

Sw. Trumpets 16', 8'
Gt. Foundations 8', 4'
Ped. 16', 8', Gt. to Ped.

Bryan Jeffery Leech
Arr. by Grimoaldo Macchia

Sw. -Tpt. 16'
+Clarion 4'
rit.
a tempo
Gt.

20
rit.
Pomposo ♩= ca. 69
22
Sw. +Mixtures
a tempo
Gt. +Foundation 2'
25
28
rit.

Prelude on

COME SHARE THE LORD

MUSIC BY
Bryan Jeffery Leech

ARRANGED FOR ORGAN BY
Grimoaldo Macchia